428·4076DAN

St. John's College
Library
Date for return

WITHDRAWN

0 8 MAY 2022

31845

D0363549

372.4

THE STANDARD READING TESTS

By the Same Authors

*

THE ROYAL ROAD READERS

Books 1-9
Miniatures
First Companion Books, etc.
Teachers' Book

LEARNING TO READ

THE PHONIC WORD METHOD

*

PROGRESS IN READING
(*Published by University of Nottingham Institute of Education*)

By J. C. Daniels

TEACHERS' HANDBOOK OF TEST CONSTRUCTION

ATTAINMENT TESTS IN PHYSICS

STATISTICAL METHODS IN EDUCATIONAL

RESEARCH

By Hunter Diack

HOW WORDS WORK

LEARNING AND TEACHING

ENGLISH GRAMMAR

THE ALPHABET WORD BOOK

THE STANDARD READING TESTS

J. C. DANIELS, B.Sc., M.Ed.

and

HUNTER DIACK, M.A.

1964

CHATTO & WINDUS

LONDON

ST. JOHN'S
COLLEGE
YORK.

PUBLISHED BY
CHATTO & WINDUS (EDUCATIONAL) LTD
42 WILLIAM IV STREET
LONDON WC2

*

CLARKE, IRWIN AND CO LTD
TORONTO

428.4076

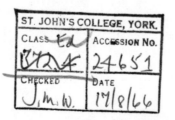

ST. JOHN'S COLLEGE, YORK.

CLASS Ed	ACCESSION No.
372.4	24651
CHECKED J.m.W.	DATE 17/8/66

FIRST PUBLISHED 1958
SECOND IMPRESSION 1960
THIRD IMPRESSION 1964

PRINTED IN GREAT BRITAIN BY
LOWE & BRYDONE (PRINTERS) LTD
LONDON
© 1958 CHATTO AND WINDUS

CONTENTS

*

THE ASSESSMENT OF READING SKILL

In recent years it has come to be generally acknowledged that in reading a number of different skills are involved.

The statement has a number of implications for the practising teacher.

Teachers need to assess their pupils' abilities not in order to affix permanent labels on them, but in order to decide what should be the next step in the teaching programme.

Teachers will realise, however, that broad, unparticularised estimations of reading ability are of little use for this purpose. The more detailed the information at his disposal, the more fertile the teaching programme can be made.

What are the particular skills which a competent reader has mastered?

Elsewhere we have defined reading as the skill of translating the letters of words, in a given order, into sounds that have meaning. This definition of the complex skills involved in reading is only a re-casting of the statement, with which few people would disagree, that the English language is written down by means of an alphabet. It is only another definition of what is meant by alphabetical writing. This definition is arrived at through purely deductive reasoning.

But when we come to analysing the nature of the psychological and physiological factors involved in reading, we must take into account the scientific facts available on human perception and thinking.

(1) *Seeing*. It is self-evident that reading involves seeing. The visual analysis of complex patterns of print is one type of analysis which must, in efficient reading, proceed in a precise and definite sequence and at an extraordinarily rapid speed. In assessing reading skills, therefore, we need information about the effectiveness of the pupils' methods of visual analysis.

(2) *Association of Sight and Sound*. A pupil who has mastered reading has learned to associate certain patterns of print (letters and groups of letters) with certain sounds and to go beyond this to the association of these patterns of sound with the ideas which they symbolise in the language. The teacher who wishes to understand her pupils' reading will want to

know how effectively these links between sight and sound have been established and whether the full process (sight $\longrightarrow$ sound $\longrightarrow$ meaning) has been arrested at the second stage, so producing the phenomena of 'barking at print' or 'word calling', i.e. when the child is satisfied with the sound and does not feel the need to go beyond the sound to the meaning. It is clear that sounds without meaning are not language.

(3) *Hearing*. Even in 'silent' reading the hearing centres of the brain are involved, at least indirectly. The child in learning to read has not only to make a visual analysis of the printed word; he has also to make an aural analysis of the sounds of which spoken words are compounded. In order to gain insight into why the printed word *MAN* says (speaks) the sound *man*, he needs not only to be able to make a visual analysis of the word *man* into *m*, *a* and *n*, but also to analyse the sound *man* into m-m-m, a-a-a and n-n-n, the noises of which the spoken word *man* is made up.

The teacher needs to know, therefore, how effective is the child's aural analysis of spoken words and how effectively he can re-synthesise them mentally into the whole word *man*—and beyond this the idea of *man*.

The reading of deaf mutes and the Braille reading of the blind in no way conflict with this analysis of reading—the analysis merely needs re-phrasing to cover these special conditions. Since speaking and hearing are interdependent activities, vocal-speech skills are involved in reading. It is quite evident that the extent of a child's vocabulary influences a child's ability in reading. We shall deal with this matter in some detail below. It is clear, however, that since in reading the child goes from sight to sound, the sound is 'produced' by the child himself. This means that the speech centres of the brain are involved in reading, even when the noises produced are sub-liminal in intensity—i.e. silent reading.

The teacher therefore needs to investigate those particular speech habits of the child which may be preventing proper progress in reading.

Before describing the battery of diagnostic tests it is necessary to make one more distinction—that between reading skill and reading experience. An example makes the matter clearer.

Suppose a child is given a card on which are printed the words—

abacus
minim
saffron
replica

The child is asked 'Which of these words is the name of a machine for helping you to do sums? Point to the word.'

He will be an exceptionally able child who can point to *abacus*, except of course by pure luck, even though he can 'read' all four words correctly. The reason for his failure will probably be that all four words are rare, and consequently not within the child's experience. His linguistic experience is too limited. Yet all four words can easily be *read* by a child who has only a fair level of reading skill in the mechanical sense of the word, for they are all simple words in the phonetic sense.

The reading tests in this battery distinguish between reading tests which are tests of reading skill (though we want also to make sure that that skill has not been arrested at the word-calling stage) and tests of linguistic and reading experience. Both types of test are included in the battery. However, the tests are primarily concerned with testing reading skills.

READING TESTS IN USE IN SCHOOLS TODAY

Two main types of reading test are widely used in schools today—word-recognition tests and comprehension tests.

(a) *Word-Recognition Tests*

These are lists of words which the child is asked to read out aloud to the tester. The words bear no meaningful relationship to one another. The words are selected for inclusion in the test on purely statistical grounds—the proportions of children at various ages reading the word correctly being the operative fact. The words in the list are arranged in order of difficulty—statistical difficulty. For example, suppose 60 per cent of 6-year-olds read *toy* correctly and 50 per cent of these same 6-year-olds read *man* correctly, *toy* is statistically an easier word to read than *man*. But in a real teaching sense, as we have demonstrated elsewhere, because *man* is regularly phonic (all the letters are pronounced and given their most common sound values), it is in another sense an easier word to read than *toy*. The reasons why *toy* may turn out statistically to be an easier word than *man* is not solely due to the degree of reading skill involved but rather to an intimate mixture of reading skill and reading experience. For reasons connected with the dominance of the whole-word methods of teaching reading, *toy* is often introduced into early reading books long before the word *man*. Therefore a young child may have met *toy* in his reading many times before he comes across the word *man*. In the grading of our tests we have abandoned the statistical method of determining a word's difficulty for a difficulty-grading in terms of degree of reading skill involved in its recognition. Naturally we have only used words that are to be found in the *spoken* vocabulary of the children being tested.

(b) *Silent Reading or Comprehension Tests*

In these tests the child is required to indicate, by some means or other, that he has silently read and understood a sentence or a passage of continuous prose. For example, the child may be given a series of questions such as the following:

'You may buy stamps at a post (man, box, office, letter).' The child is asked to underline the one word in brackets which completes the sentence sensibly. These questions are then arranged in their statistical order of difficulty.

READING AGES

One important feature of most modern reading tests concerns the method of recording the scores. The words in word-recognition tests or the questions in comprehension tests, as has been explained, are arranged in order of difficulty and then, again on the basis of purely statistical evidence, each word or question is ascribed a *Reading Age rating*. For example, in Schonell's word-recognition test *playing* is given a 5·9 years rating and *pivot* a 11·8 years rating.

The child reads through the list until he has made ten successive errors, after which the testing is suspended. The total Reading Age allocations of the words read correctly are added up, giving an overall Reading Age of one-tenth of a year per word plus 5 years. This Reading Age may then be compared with his chronological age and the degree of his backwardness or precocity established.

There are certain advantages in the method. The Reading Age method enables an individual child's performance on the test to be compared with the average performance on the same test of other children throughout the country. Suppose a child has a Reading Age of 7 years 1 month. This means that he can read correctly exactly the same number of words in the test as the average 7-year-1-month-old child throughout the country.

Teachers have come to regard this universal measure of comparison as helpful, and for this reason the main test in this series has been carefully standardised and a table provided translating raw test marks into Reading Ages is given. There are, however, a number of serious weaknesses in the

Reading Age method of recording a child's achievement. We can deal here with only one of these weaknesses.

The Reading Age method compares the achievement of a particular child with the average achievement of other children throughout the country. The concept of 'average' hides the fact that in a country like Britain individual schools are making widely different approaches to, and laying different emphases on, the teaching of reading. To take the most obvious example. Suppose one group of children, Group A, has been led towards reading by introducing to it gradually, by 'Look and Say' methods,[1] a basic sight vocabulary of, say, 200 words. This basic sight vocabulary will usually consist of common and 'interesting' words. It will almost certainly contain words with complex spelling. Let us assume that the average 6-year-old in this group can recognise 100 of these sight words in a word-recognition test. Let us suppose now that another group of children, Group B, has begun reading by the old-fashioned phonic method leading on to reading sentences such as 'The cat sat on the mat'. These children will, let us assume, on the average be able to read, at the age of 6, 100 out of 200 words of simple phonic construction—i.e. of the *cat*, *dog*, *rat* type.

Let us now give both groups of children a word-recognition test. If the first words of the test are 'common' and 'interesting' words, Group A will score higher than Group B, whereas if the first words in the test are of simple phonetic structure, Group B will score higher than Group A.

It is thus obvious that a child's score on any reading test depends not only upon his 'reading ability' and on the statistically-averaged 'difficulty' of the words in the test, but also upon the relation of method of teaching used to the particular words included in the test.

Suppose we now combine the scores of Groups A and B in this test and give the test to a group, C. Can any relevant information be obtained by comparing Group C's performance in the test with the combined average of Groups A and B? The Reading Age method appears to do so, but only by masking highly complicated processes behind simple averages. For example the scores of 30 or 40 different groups may be averaged to give the norms.

The second objection to the Reading Age method of recording test results and of the purely statistical method of constructing and arranging reading tests is that the 'reading age' gives no *direct* help to the teacher in deciding what particular treatment the child needs. If a teacher knows

---

[1] i.e. by a method which does not give the child any direct suggestion as to the method of making a meaningful visual analysis of the structure of words.

that an 8-year-old child has a reading age of 6½ years, she knows that compared to the 'average' child he is backward. However, this knowledge does not tell the teacher how and why he is backward, nor does it indicate what special difficulties he is meeting with and what exercises he needs to go on to next.

The teacher needs a test (or series of tests) which will indicate whether the child is backward and will show what the child's actual standard or degree of mastery of reading skill is. She wants information concerning the special difficulties the child is faced with, and on the basis of this information she needs some indication as to what the next steps are in improving the child's reading ability. The battery of reading tests collected on this book have been specifically designed to provide the teacher with information of this sort. The usual type of Word Recognition test is known to give statistically imprecise estimates of reading ability at the earliest stages (5–7 years range).[1] Yet it is just in this range that teachers find the need for full and precise information. In constructing the Standard Reading Tests, we have paid particular attention to this point.

For example, to achieve a Reading Age of 7 years on one well-known Word Recognition test, the child has to read only 20 different words whilst on the Standard Test of Reading Skill, to achieve the same Reading Age, he has to read 68 different words, each chosen to assess a specific aspect of reading skill. Accordingly, the Standard Reading Test estimates of reading ability are on a finer scale of grading and the corresponding Reading Ages are, statistically, more reliable at the earliest levels of reading.

Some teachers who use the tests may wonder why no precise norms and Achievement Ages are given for any of the tests except the Standard Test of Reading Skill, the Spelling Test and the Reading Experience Test. The reason is that the others are tests of skills which *must* be completely mastered if normal progress is to be made. Therefore, except where otherwise indicated in the introductory notes to the separate tests, pupils are expected to give 80–100 per cent correct answers.

[1] G. F. Reed: "Reading Test for Hull". *Studies in Education (University College of Hull)* Vol. II, No. 1, 1953. See also *Reading Ability*, Ministry of Education Pamphlet No. 18, 1950, Appendix B.

THE BATTERY OF STANDARD TESTS

THE battery consists of twelve tests, each with a specific function to perform. Test No. 1, called the Standard Test of Reading Skill, is the key test of the battery. This is the test which has been designed to be given to every child who, it is evident, has not fully mastered all the skills involved in reading.

In assessing a child's results on the Standard Test of Reading Skill, the examiner will note that most children, when their age and past educational history are taken into account, are making satisfactory progress and are showing no abnormal features in their development. A record should then be made of these children's reading ages and reading standards and no further tests need to be given to these children. This will be the normal practice with the majority of children—a regular six-monthly testing on the Standard Test.

Other children's performances on the Standard Test, however, will cause the teacher some concern. She may notice that a particular child has not kept pace with the rest of his class and that he has made little progress since the last testing; he continues to make errors involving incorrect recognition of some letters—or he guesses at words from the first letters—or he confuses *b*'s and *d*'s. When the teacher comes across a child showing these characteristics as he does the Standard Test, he will conclude that this child needs to be given one or more of the other tests in the battery—i.e. to be given one or more of the diagnostic tests. To help teachers to use the battery of tests successfully, full, detailed notes accompany each test and sub-test.

The other tests in the battery are as follows:

Test No. 2. Copying Abstract Figures
This is a test designed to discover something about the child's perceptual development and of his hand-eye co-ordination.

Test No. 3. Copying a Sentence
This test is basically a more difficult version of Test No. 2. It will tell the teacher something of the child's experience in seeing and copying letters.

Test No. 4. Visual Discrimination and Orientation Test

This test is designed to determine more exactly what the child sees when he looks at pictures, diagrams and letters and to pick out those children who have not yet reached the stage of perceiving with left-right orientation, an important principle of identity.

Test No. 5. Letter-Recognition Test

The letters of the alphabet are here printed in a special order, with detailed test items to discover the degree of skill in letter-recognition.

Test No. 6. Aural Discrimination Test

This test has been designed to help the teacher discover how acute is the aural discrimination of a child when he listens to words.

Test No. 7. Diagnostic Word-Recognition Tests
    (A) Two-letter and three-letter phonically simple words
    (B) Words with duo-consonantal blends at the beginning
    (C) Words with duo-consonantal blends at the end
    (D) Polysyllabic phonically simple words
    (E) Words involving all the main rules of phonetic spelling in English
    (F) The commonest irregularly spelt words
    (G) 'Reversible' words
    (H) Three- and four-letter nonsense syllables (to be used with caution)

Test No. 8. Oral Word-Recognition Test

This test is designed to discover something about the child's ear-eye co-ordination. The child has to recognise in print words spoken by the teacher.

Test No. 9. Picture Word-Recognition Test

This tests the ability of the child to choose from amongst other words the names of pictured objects.

Test No. 10. Silent Prose Reading and Comprehension Test

This is a test of comprehension of a passage of prose.

Test No. 11. Graded Spelling Test

A carefully graded and standardised test of spelling, broken up into four sub-tests.

Test No. 12. Graded Test of Reading Experience

This is a test, for children who score very highly in the Standard Test of Reading Skill, of the extent to which reading skills have been used in practice. It is as much a vocabulary test as a reading test.

THE STANDARD TEST OF READING SKILL

Description of the Test

IN essence the test is a word-recognition test—the children read out aloud a series of items, printed one item per page. It is, however, different from the usual word-recognition test for two reasons. Unlike those word-recognition tests which consist of a list of words bearing no meaningful relation with one another, the Standard Test consists of a series of 36 sentences in question form. This means that sometimes the children can get some help in word-recognition from the context—or more exactly from the form of sentence. Moreover, it ensures that the children do not concentrate on mere word-recognition or 'word-calling'. Each sentence has meaning. The questions have been carefully chosen so that once they have been read correctly, the child is almost certain to give the right answer. The importance of this is that the child reads the question aloud but concentrates on getting at its meaning—for he is anxious to give the right answer. The children in fact always believe that they are being marked on the answers to the questions, not on their reading. Marks are not given for correct answers to the questions, but the children are not informed of this. Because of the help given by the context of the question and by the meaningful setting in which the reading aloud is done, the results on this test give a true reflection of a child's mastery of the skill of reading.

The construction of the 36 test items and the order in which they are presented to the child is of crucial importance. The order of the items, as already mentioned, is not only a statistical order but also a real order of difficulty based upon the degree of phonic complexity of the words making up the question. The first question, '*Can a dog run?*' is easier to read than No. 16, '*Can a chicken see?*' There is little difference in the frequency with which all these words occur in the English language, as given by the Thorndike Word List. Moreover, when these two questions were given *orally* we found no statistically significant difference in the proportion of children giving the correct answers. The two questions are, however, placed in the test as No. 1 and No. 16 respectively because '*Can a chicken see?*' contains two second-level phonic rules— the digraphs *ch* and *ee* and a duo-syllabic word '*chicken*'. In spite of the fact that the questions were placed in a particular order on *a priori* grounds, experimentally No. 1 was found statistically to be easier to read than No. 16. Experiment has shown that the *a priori* order of difficulty coincides very closely with the statistical order of difficulty throughout the entire test.[1]

This system of ordering the items, however, has made it possible to use an additional and diagnostically more helpful method of recording the result than that of Reading Ages—the method of Reading Standards. Full details are given in the section, 'Assessment of the Test Results' (see p. 19). This alternative method of recording the level of skill achieved is based on the theory of qualitative stages in the growth of skills. When reading ability is tested by using a word-recognition test which has been built up by the method of statistical selection of words, the scores inevitably suggest a gradual and steady growth of power of word-recognition, with no qualitative breaks. This even, continuous growth is, however, only a necessary consequence of the sort of test being used. Such tests hide the fact that there are recognisable qualitative stages in the development of reading ability. For example, as soon as a child grasps that *ch*, *th* and *sh* usually stand for four definite sounds, a whole series of new words is immediately available to him. In other words, his reading ability enters a new qualitative phase.

After careful deliberation it was decided to emphasize the qualitative factor in the development of reading ability by reverting to the old term of Reading Standards. The meaning of Reading Standards is fully described later. It is important to note here, however, that if the child has reached a particular Reading Standard, it is possible to *describe* which particular reading skills he has mastered and, hence, to deduce something about those skills he has still to master. This would be quite impossible if only a Reading Age was available.

To whom the Test should be given

The Standard Test of Reading Skill (Test No. 1) should be given to all children still in the primary stage of reading (i.e. with reading ages up to 9 years) at regular intervals of six months or a year.

How to give the Test

The tester will find it simplifies the task of recording errors, of giving marks and of assessing the quality of the child's reading if the test

[1] See *Progress in Reading*, p. 13, and J. C. Daniels' "Testing Reading Ability" (*Forward Trends in the Treatment of the Backward Child*, Vol. II, No. 3, 1957).

questions, serially numbered, are cyclostyled on two sides of a quarto page. One sheet is used for each child. The child's name, his age, class and any other personal details that may be required, are entered on the cyclostyled page. As the child reads the test materials from the printed pages of the book, each question is ticked (if read correctly) or, when errors are made, the erroneous reply is written in over the word in the test. It will be found to be of no value to record the reply to the question the child makes since practically every child gets them all right.

The best position for testing is at a table. The tester should seat the child to his right, round the corner of the table.

Questions 1-26. Place the book before the child and open the page at Question 1—'Can a dog run?'

Say 'Read this aloud for me'—pointing to the sentence. As soon as the child has read the question say—'Well, can it?' Usually he will answer 'Yes'. Agree with him, showing pleasure at his success. The child will almost certainly reply immediately with a grin. If he looks puzzled, say 'Read it again'. Repeat the same procedure until he grasps that he has to read the question out aloud, understand it and finally answer it.

Turn over the page to No. 2 and repeat the same procedure. Soon, if he can read the question, he will answer without prompting and usually show a good deal of pleasure in doing so.

When a child fails to read any word or reads it incorrectly, he should be helped or corrected. He may be told, for example, 'Try this word again' (pointing) or 'Try to build the word up'. Often, however, it will be better simply to tell the child what a particular word is, if he hesitates silently for more than ten seconds. When a word has had to be corrected (unprompted self-corrections are, of course, allowable) that item must be recorded as a 'failure'.

Questions 27-36. Let the child read the question, and then interrupt and say 'Now read all these'—pointing to the four possible answers. Ask 'Which of these words is the right one?' and the child will almost certainly give the right answer. Go on to say this: 'In these next questions I want you to read out aloud the question, then read out aloud all the four possible answers and then tell me the right answer'.

When to stop the Testing

Discontinue the testing as soon as the child has failed to score at least 3 marks on any 3 *consecutive* questions. (For Marking Key, see the next section.)

B

For example, a child scores 3 marks each for questions Nos. 1-16, zero for 17, 3 for 18, 19, 20, 21, 22, zero for 23, 3 for 24 and 25, zero for 26, 2 for 27, 1 for 28. Testing is then discontinued.

MARKING KEY

Questions 1-26. Three marks are given for each question read out fully correct. Zero marks are given for any question in which the child makes one or more errors. Zero marks are given for a question in which he pauses for so long that he has to be told one or more words.

Questions 27-36. One mark is given for each *question* read correctly and one mark *each* for each possible *answer* read correctly. This makes the maximum mark for each question in this section five marks.

Maximum Marks for the whole test is 128.

N.B.—Marks are not added or subtracted for right or wrong answers to the actual questions. Most children who score full marks on an item also answer the question correctly. When a wrong answer is given, however, stop to correct the child in a friendly way.

Table of Reading Ages

To find the child's Reading Age from the sum of his marks on the whole test, consult Table 1. Look in the body of the table for the child's total score or next highest score appearing in the table. Then read off the Reading Age in years. (*N.B.*—A Reading Age of 7·1 years = $7\frac{1}{10}$ years; NOT 7 years 1 month.)

TABLE I

Years	·0	·1	·2	·3	·4	·5	·6	·7	·8	·9
5·0	—	—	3	6	9	12	15	18	21	24
6·0	27	30	33	36	39	42	45	51	54	57
7·0	60	63	66	70	74	77	80	84	87	90
8·0	94	97	100	103	107	110	114	117	120	124
9·0	127									

For example, a child scores 82 marks. The next highest score appearing in the table is 84. The Reading Age (R.A.) is therefore 7·7 years—or 7 years 8 months.

Reading Quotients

To obtain a Reading Quotient (R.Q.), find the child's Chronological Age (C.A.) in years. (*N.B.*—convert Chronological Age given in years and months to decimals, e.g. 7 y. 11 m. = 7·9 years.) Substitute R.A. and C.A. in this formula:

$$R.Q. = \frac{R.A.}{C.A.} \times 100$$

(Mean R.Q. = 100 Standard Deviation of R.Q.'s = 12·1).

Reading Standard

The child's score on the Standard Test of Reading Skill should now be transposed into a Reading Standard, for which purpose Table II should be used.

TABLE II

CONVERSION OF TEST MARKS INTO READING STANDARDS

Mark Range	Reading Standard
0-6	O
9-15	I
18-27	II
30-42	III
45-78	IV
79-108	V
109	VI

ASSESSMENT OF THE TEST RESULTS

A detailed, qualitative, diagnostic interpretation of the responses is now necessary to decide if special remedial treatment is required and what form that remedial treatment should take. Qualitative interpretation is an art which the teacher gains by judiciously blending teaching experience and the scientific understanding of the nature of the skills involved in fluent reading. The following notes are offered as an elementary guide to the beginner.

It is clear that a child aged 5·0 years who records Reading Standard O is in a somewhat different category from the 9-year-old boy who also has a Reading Standard of zero. The former may have a Reading

Quotient of, approximately, 100 whilst the second has a Reading Quotient of only, approximately, 60.

The differences between them obviously do not lie in the differences in levels of mastery of reading skills. The main difference is usually in attitude to learning—the older child being quite differently motivated in approaching new 'reading' activities from the 5-year-old. This means that often both children will need the same types of exercise. The mode of presentation will, however, need to be very different. This should always be borne in mind when interpreting a child's Reading Standard.

Reading Standard O (R.A. 5·0 years–5·3 years)

Children who record a Reading Standard of zero are children who have very little functionally-operative reading ability. They are still illiterate. This does not mean that they have not reached a level of proficiency in one or more of the skills necessary to begin reading. Children at zero standard in reading still differ enormously in their readiness to begin learning to read effectively.

All Standard O children should be given the following Diagnostic Reading Tests:

> Test 2. Copying Abstract Figures.
> Test 3. Copying a Sentence.
> Test 4. Visual Discrimination and Orientation Test.
> Test 5. Letter-Recognition Test.
> Test 6. Aural Discrimination Test.

From these tests a pattern of the specific deficiencies will probably emerge. If the child scores reasonably well in all these five tests, then he is ready to begin a consistent course, along the lines of *Royal Road Readers* Book I.

Difficulties with Tests 2, 3 and 4 suggest a child who has been starved of pre-primary work, drawing, tracing, looking at and interpreting pictures. In addition to this the matching exercises of *Royal Road Readers* Book I,[1] together with other visual matching exercises the teacher can prepare herself, will prove invaluable.

Success with Test 5 would indicate a degree of mastery of letter skills in advance of his reading ability. These children need word-blending exercises, using especially such words as *man, miss, sum,* whose consonants are *continuous* labials and sibilants.

---

[1] And the same materials in apparatus form published by Messrs. Philip & Tacey.

Reading Standard I (R.A. 5·4 years–5·6 years)

This stage of learning to read is quite fundamental to all future development.

If a child scores 15 marks, i.e. successfully tackles sentences as difficult as 'Is the sun wet?', he has gone a long way along the road towards insight into the nature of alphabetic writing. There is a fairly high degree of understanding that letters stand for sounds and of the fact that the order of letters in words is important.

The child, however, has now to move on to (or perhaps is having difficulty in grasping) some of the consonantal blends. It is also possible that syllabisation is providing some difficulty.

The child should therefore be given Tests 7A, 7B, 7C, 7D, 8 and 9.

These diagnostic tests will show more precisely where the child's difficulty lies and will suggest to the teacher exercises for helping the child to reach the next Reading Standard. Lists of words beginning and ending with the blends may be useful, but these lists can easily be overdone. It is not uncommon for the child reading such lists to establish a habit of looking at the whole of the first word of the list and subsequently looking only at the initial letters of the other words. This is particularly true of blends at the ends of words since these lists will often turn out to be rhyming lists. (See *Progress in Reading*, pp. 48-49.)

The results from Test 8 will show whether the child has any specific auditory difficulties. These often affect the skill of analysing certain consonantal blends. Slight speech defects have their influence on performance in Test 9. Both hearing and speech difficulties (and here is meant only those very specific and peculiarly individual defects, not gross hearing and speech deficiencies) can be corrected by suitable exercises in listening and speaking.

Reading Standard II (R.A. 5·7 years–6·0 years)

Children who reach Reading Standard II are well on the way to mastery of the most important reading skills. They now 'know' the letters functionally, in words, and can recognise quite complex consonantal blends.

The cause of failure in the items of the Standard Test in the next higher standard is usually difficulty with *syllabisation*. It is also possible that difficulty is being experienced with the 'special' words, i.e. with the common non-phonically spelt words like *be, do, all*. Children at Reading Standard II should therefore be given Tests 7A, 7B, 7C, 7D.

From the results of these tests it should be possible to evaluate the nature of the difficulties with which the child is now confronted.

Experiment shows that the majority of children are able to take in their stride the short and common 'special' or non-phonic words if, when they meet them in their reading for the first time, they do so with a fair degree of understanding of the principles of alphabetic writing. In *Progress in Reading* it is shown that after reading ability has passed above a certain point (approximately Standard II) children then make very rapid progress in remembering and reading these common special words.

A very few children, however, do find difficulty with these special words. They can develop into stubborn 'hard-core' cases—apparently refusing to admit of any 'phonetic' principles other than the simplest rules they have already learned. It is no remedy to give repeated 'Look and Say' (i.e. unexplained) presentations of these 'special' words; even the most stubborn cases can be cured by patient explanation on the teacher's part.

Children are intensely rational people and it is our adult spelling that is irrational—not the child. If it is explained that these 'special' words are 'funny' words, i.e. words which break the rules, and if the letters in the words which do have their usual sounds (and there are always some) are pointed out, they then remember these words as exceptions. Children respond to the teacher's confidences. This is perhaps the best advice that can be given to the teacher to help her to deal with difficulties of this sort.

It is usual to teach the alphabetic names of the letters before this stage is reached. Test 5 will reveal whether they have learned these.

Difficulties with syllabisation can be treated by means of exercises designed to help children to see two syllables in longer words. Lists of duo-syllabic words in which both syllables may be pronounced independently should be used. The breaks between the syllables should be indicated by spaces between the syllables greater than ordinary letter spaces but less than word spaces. Hyphens do not help.

Some children find great difficulty in pronouncing syllables which, on their own, are nonsense. It is remarkable how firm a grasp of phonics a child must have before he will entrust himself to 'read' Test 7H. With a number of children, though it must be used with discretion, Test 7H will provide some valuable information.

Children who have reached Reading Standard II need plenty of practice with properly graded readers, e.g. *Royal Road Readers: Miniatures 1-8.*

Reading Standard III (R.A. 6·1 years–6·5 years)

Children in Reading Standard III are at a critical stage of learning the skills involved in reading. They have already achieved a fairly high degree of understanding of the fundamentals of reading; they have grasped the fact that there are a number of exceptions to the rules—'special' words. They have now to add to their repertoire the full list of more complex phonic 'rules', beginning with such diagraphs as *th*, *oo* and *or*. There are also the rules about the distant modification of vowels, e.g. *cap* becoming *cape*, the sound of the *a* being modified by the distant *e*, whilst the *e* itself is not pronounced.

The test most useful here is Test 7E, the test which ranges over all these phonic rules. Tests 8 and 9 should also be given at this stage.

For the younger children who are making steady progress in learning to read and who have now reached Reading Standard III, further graded reading material, following on lessons and exercises designed to teach these more complex phonic rules, is usually enough. A few children, however, seem to stagnate for a considerable time at this stage. This stagnation is often caused by encouraging the children to try to read ungraded material, i.e. material which contains simple ideas but in words which are complicated, phonically speaking. Such reading is often not helpful.

With these children, it is often necessary to go back again to material at the level of Standard II so that the child may regain his confidence in his ability to read. Then slowly, with the aid of apparatus such as, for example, the Hemming Word Wheels,[1] introduce the new phonic rules, one or two at a time. Double *o* (*oo*) and double *e* (*ee*) are the easiest digraphs for them to understand.

> *Reversals.* In Standards I, II and III the phenomena of reversals may be observed in some children. There are several types of 'reversal' reading: (1) the confusion of *b* and *d*; (2) reading certain words backwards, i.e. right to left, of which the classical example is *was* read as *saw*; (3) mirror *writing* of various types. Whenever any sort of 'reversal' turns up, give Tests 2, 3, 7G and 11A. Treatment of reversal errors is discussed in the section 'Assessment of the Test Results', on p. 165.

Reading Standard IV (R.A. 6·6 years–7·6 years)

Children who have reached Reading Standard IV have mastered most of the basic skills in reading. What they need most of all now is a great

---

[1] *A Book of Handy Words*, James Hemming (Longmans).

deal of controlled practice with graded material together with some written work. This written work needs to be carefully planned. Too much 'free' work at this stage sometimes helps to 'fix' bad spelling of some important words.

Children at Reading Standard IV may sometimes usefully be given Tests 10 and 12—particularly if there is any suspicion that the mechanics of reading have been achieved at the expense of 'reading for meaning'. Children whose Reading Experience Ages on Test 12 are considerably less than their Reading Ages as given by the Standard Test need work on graded exercises in comprehension. These exercises may be devised along the lines of Tests 10 and 12.

Reading Standards V and VI (R.A. 7·6 years–9·0 years)

Children whose reading is at this level have effectively mastered all the skills of reading. All they now require is wider reading experience. The extent of this experience will be partly reflected in the scores on Test 12.

The children who record Reading Standard VI have reached such a degree of familiarity with the printed forms of all the commoner words that it is no longer necessary for them to make a *complete* visual analysis in reading these words, though careful analysis will still be necessary, as it is for adults, with unfamiliar words. These children have now reached the stage of maintaining an efficient balance between the clues provided by the context and those provided by parts of the printed word itself. It is in this connection that the rather vague phrase 'seeing words as wholes' can be said to have some precision of meaning. Contextual clues, which at the earliest stages of reading may be so confusing to the child (particularly if the reading materials used over-encourage reliance on context) now come to be of real positive value in the acquisition of reading fluency. The Standard Test does not give reading ages above nine years since beyond this level a different type of reading test, the Graded Test of Reading Experience (Test 12), is required.

TEST 1

THE STANDARD TEST
OF READING SKILL

Which of these would a car go over to cross a river?

        a garage

        a grocer

        a road bridge

        a railway siding

Have birds three legs?

Can a dog run?

Has a cat legs?

Has a cup a lid?

Is an egg red?

Is the sun wet?

Can a top spin?

Can a fox run fast?

Can a duck swim?

Is a red flag black?

Has a camel a hump on its back?

Is a windmill an animal?

Is a robin kept in a kennel?

Can string be cut?

Do bells ring?

Have all trees roots?

Can a chicken see?

Do fish feed on grass?

Are books often kept on shelves?

Can a bus go too fast for a man to keep up with it?

Do farmers use tractors?

Does a goose look like a big duck?

Can dinner plates be broken?

Are skates made of steel?

Can you catch whales with a rod and line?

Is white the opposite of black?

Which of these do you use at dinner-time?

a rope

a fork

a frame

a park

Which of these is a farm animal?

a goal
a house
a horse
a sheet

Which of these can be read?

an oak beam

a hockey team

a daily paper

a loaf of bread

Which of these would you keep in your money box?

saddles

coins

joints

battles

Which of the following would you find in a grocer's shop?

        rowing boats
        growing crops
        dried peas
        fried fish

Which of the following would you be likely to see in the window of a shop that sells supplies for gardeners?

packets of soap powder

wild flowers

packets of flower seeds

country houses

Which of these can be found on the sea-shore?

ripe pears

open doors

rounded pebbles

moorland fires

Which of these is used by gardeners?

    automatic washing machines

    lawn mowers

    faulty refrigerators

    beautiful pictures

Which of these can usually be bought at the chemist's?

        dough-mixing machines

        writing paper

        cough mixture

        physical energy

TEST 2

COPYING ABSTRACT FIGURES

To whom this Test should be given

(1) All children who record Grade O on the Standard Test of Reading Skill.

(2) Those children who, it is suspected, have difficulty in left-right orientation and who as a result of this frequently confuse certain individual letters and misread certain words where left-right orientation is specially involved.

(3) Those children whose eye-hand co-ordination and hand motor-control seem to be impaired.

How to give the Test

Give the child a sheet of plain paper and a pencil. Place the page of Figures 1-4 before him and cover up, with a sheet of paper, Figures 2, 3 and 4. Pointing now to Figure 1 say 'Can you copy this for me?' 'Copy it for me on this paper here with this pencil.' When this job has been completed to the child's satisfaction say 'Yes—that's very good—now see if you can copy this one'. (Uncover Figure 2.) Do not make any comment on the child's efforts except to say 'Yes, that's good, go on'. Let the child attempt to copy all four figures in the same way. A few children will show some hesitation as if they do not quite understand what is wanted. When this happens, the examiner should take the pencil from the child and, in front of him, copy Figure 1. Then say 'Now you do that—make a copy of this'. Provide the child with a clean sheet of paper and hand him the pencil again.

The examiner will find it helpful to make notes on how the child **tackles** the job—which lines he draws first and the general efficiency of his **paper-and-pencil work.**

The overwhelming majority of children who score higher than Grade O on the Standard Test of Reading Skill have no difficulty whatsoever in reproducing recognisable copies of Figures 1, 2 and 3, though Figure 4, of course, presents more difficult. The child's performance should be looked at from two aspects—accuracy and 'neatness'.

Accuracy

By this is meant the interrelation of the detailed parts, the proportions, the overall size, the orientation. Here are four typical attempts.

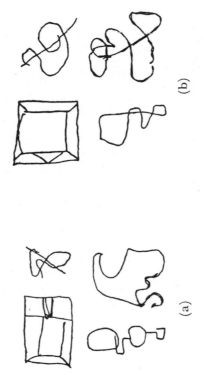

(a)

(b)

(a) shows an inability to perceive, at a level of perception high enough to direct the hand, the interrelation of the detailed parts. The proportions also are wrong and, in a sense, there is a confusion of left-right orientation. This is a very poor effort and a child with this level of performance needs a good deal of pre-reading work of a practical-manual

(c)

(d)

type—designed to help him to develop his perceptual-discriminative ability. There is little use trying to teach this child to read until his performance in this task improves.

(b) is a typical 'young' child's effort. The only thing that is wrong is that each figure is a mirror image of the original. Training in left-right discrimination, e.g. with form-board materials such as those designed by Dr. E. Newson,[1] will often work wonders with younger children. The child should be asked to try again, holding the pencil in the other hand. Often this produces the 'correct' response but the examiner should be chary of jumping to the conclusion that, for some reason or other, the child is using the wrong hand. This, however, may be so.

(c) is simply wrongly proportioned. This indicates lack of familiarity with the job of paper-and-pencil work. There is nothing in this performance which more practice will not cure.

(d) is a typical effort of the child on the border-line of being ready to read. The copies are not so disorganised as may be thought on first inspection. An effort of this sort does indicate that more hand-eye co-ordination exercises would be helpful.

'Neatness'

The second aspect from which the drawings should be looked at is 'neatness'. Most of the 'accuracy' failures will be rather untidy efforts. The untidiness of the sketches adds little information of value to the teacher. A number of drawings, however, may be basically accurate but so lacking in 'neatness' as to indicate very poor control of the hand. Most of this is due to lack of directed experience in using the pencil. It is noticeable, however, that children whose 'neatness' improves also usually improve in their ability to recognise letters and words.

Attempt (e) shows a typical 'border-line' success. Anything worse than this should be considered as worthy of the teacher's special attention.

If the examiner is doubtful about the quality of the child's performance on the test, he should give Tests 3 and 4.

[1] The Development of Line Figure Discrimination in Pre-School Children, E. Newson (Ph.D. Thesis, University of Nottingham, 1955).

(e)

TEST 2

COPYING ABSTRACT FIGURES

TEST 3

COPYING A SENTENCE

To whom this Test should be given

(1) Children who record Standard O in the Standard Test of Reading Skill.

(2) Children who are border-line 'successes' and 'failures' in Test 2.

(3) Pupils who in the Standard Test of Reading Skill appear to be guessing at many words by concentrating attention on only part of the words.

(4) Pupils who only just succeed in getting into Standard I on the Standard Test of Reading Skill.

How to give the Test

Give the child a sheet of lined paper and pencil. Then put the picture of the dog and the sentence in front of the child and say 'Look at the picture. What is that?' (pointing to the dog)—'Yes—a dog—and what is he doing?' 'Yes, he is sitting in his box.' 'Now, can you read this sentence?' pointing along the two rows of the sentence. If the child cannot read the sentence or cannot complete it easily—read it out to him, pointing to the words as they are read out. 'Now copy this sentence for me—on here', pointing to the piece of paper. Some children might begin drawing the picture of the dog but interrupt them and say 'No—don't draw the picture—copy down the words in the sentence' (pointing).

ASSESSMENT OF THE TEST RESULTS

Most of the children will be able to do this test easily. Children who show great difficulty and clumsiness in writing it have obviously little experience of writing and copying. One of the most significant things to note is the absence (or reduction to minute size) of the spaces between the words. This often indicates that these children have not in their reading (and sometimes in their speaking) come to recognise spoken words as units—a fact which the child has to learn from experience and which therefore needs to be taught.

The standard of accuracy is usually high but 'neatness' (particularly regularity and proportions of letter parts) is often very low. The remarks on 'neatness' given in the assessment of the results of Test 2 apply here in the same measure, though, if the child is reading tolerably well and the standard of 'neatness' in writing is very low, some special motor disability may be present. This may, if very marked, need specialist attention.

TEST 3

COPYING A SENTENCE

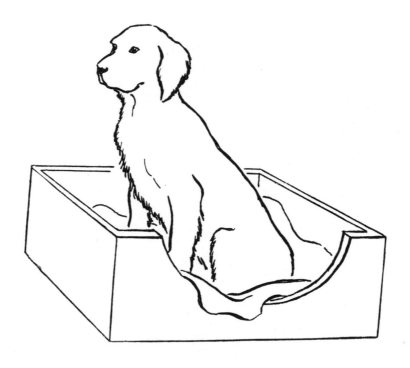

The dog sits in his box

VISUAL DISCRIMINATION AND ORIENTATION TEST

To whom the Test should be given

(1) Children who score Standard O on the Standard Test of Reading Skill.

(2) Children for whom the results of Tests 2 and 3 suggest some deficiency in left-right orientation.

(3) Children who make errors in the Standard Test of Reading Skill which suggest that the child either confuses mirror-image letters or the left-right order of letters in words.

How to give the Test

It should be noticed that the first two items are intended to introduce with easy examples the form of the questions. It is useless proceeding with the test until it is evident that the child really understands what he has to do. Put the book in front of the child and provide him with an unsharpened pencil for pointing. Point to the chair in the left margin and say, 'See this? What is it?' 'Yes—a chair. Now (*pointing along the row*) can you find another chair just like that one? Point to it.'

'Yes—that's good. Now the next one. Look at this row. Can you point to the picture of a man exactly like this one along here? Yes! Why did you choose that one and not this?' The child will probably say 'Well, this one hasn't got a hat on.' If he makes a mistake, try to explain the mistake, or encourage him to find out himself why he has made a mistake. When he really grasps what he has to do, say 'Now look at this policeman—which of these policemen is exactly the same as this one?' Note the answer. Say 'Now this line—find me something along here exactly like this one.' Give all the items in the same way.

ASSESSMENT OF THE TEST RESULTS

Visual discrimination and orientation is not something which, Topsy-like, just grows. Children have to *learn to see*. So if a child scores badly on this test, it does not necessarily mean that there is some congenital defect in his visual centres—rather that he has not had enough experience of the meaningful analysis either of pictures or of abstract diagrams. Modern infant-method books describe many types of activity (most of which can easily be adapted for older pupils) which help the child to look, to make detailed visual analyses and to give meaning to these analyses.

There are a number of items in which left-right orientation is crucial. Special attention should be paid to children who show considerable confusion in these items. The results of Tests 2 and 3 should be considered in relationship to performance on these items. The 'handedness' of the pupil may have some connexion here though this connexion will nearly always be well hidden. The relationship between handedness and difficulty in left-right orientation is not a direct one. Further enquiry, however, will sometimes establish a history where either parent or teacher has insisted upon a change of 'handedness' from the 'preferred' to the 'not-preferred' hand. It is difficult in these cases to decide whether he should now revert to the 'preferred' hand. There is no general rule in cases of this sort.

TEST 4

VISUAL DISCRIMINATION AND
ORIENTATION TEST

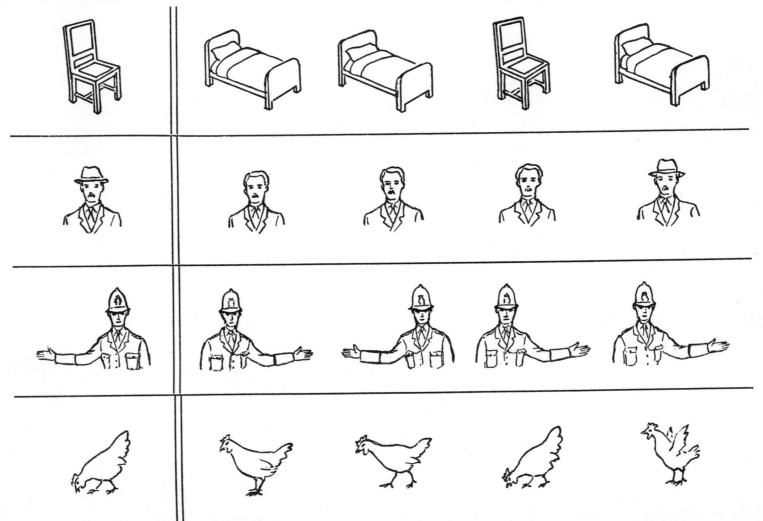

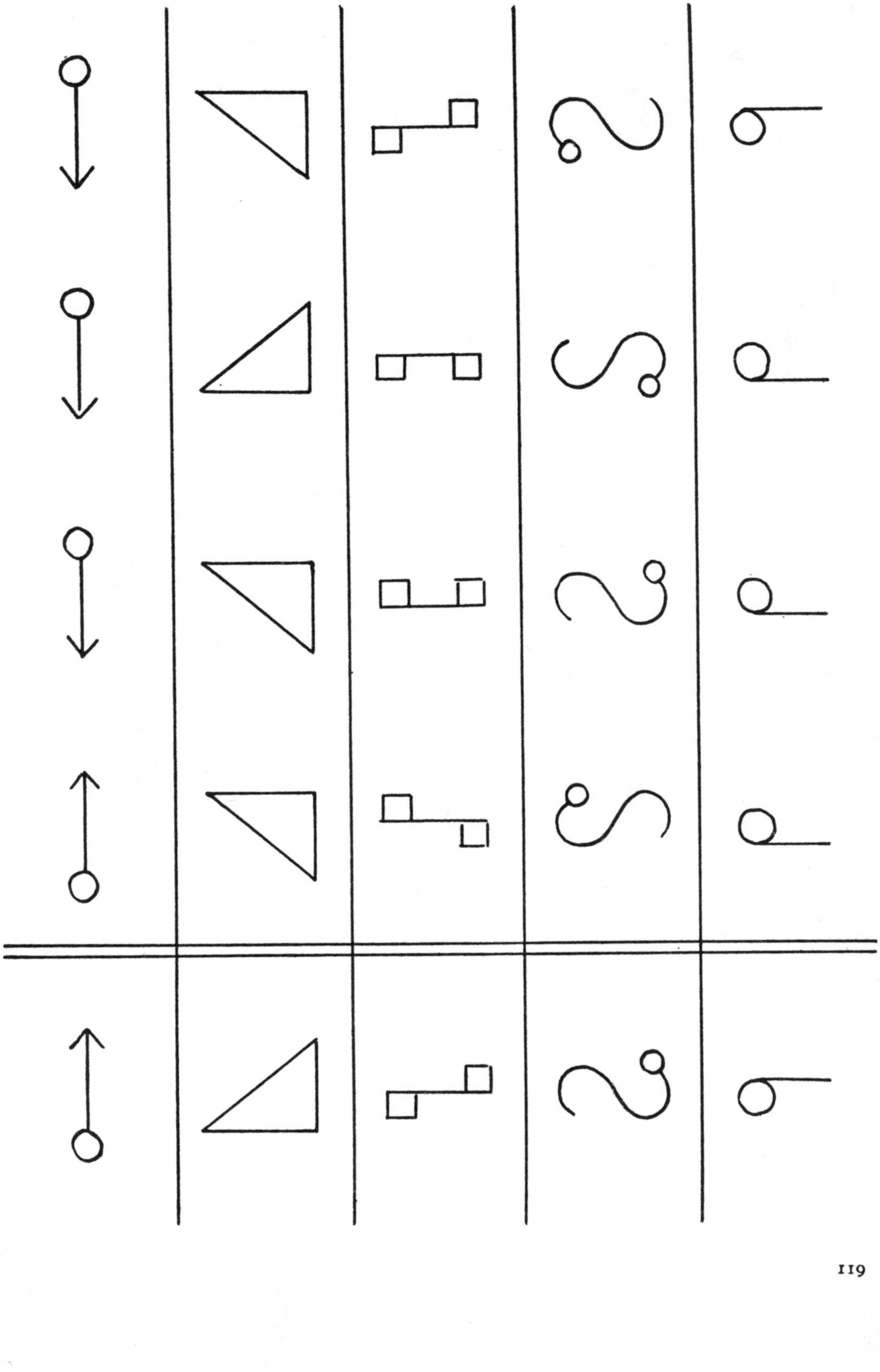

b	d	d	b	d
V	W	A	V	M
do	bo	bo	bo	do
on	an	on	am	om
wn	vn	wn	bwm	wv

dpb	bpd	dpd	dpb	dqb
swzc	szwc	swzc	scwz	czws
laos	soal	laso	loas	laos
piece	peice	pieec	piece	pceie
amnow	anmow	amnow	omnaw	awnom

LETTER-RECOGNITION TEST

To whom this Test should be given

(1) Those children who, in the Standard Test of Reading Skill, score Standard O or Standard I and who seem to have no firm grasp of the letters and their sounds.

(2) Those children who give wrong sound-values to particular letters in the Standard Test. This sometimes happens with children who score relatively highly on the Standard Test as a whole.

How to give the Test

This test material can be used in three different ways.

(a) Ask the child to give the alphabetic names of the letters reading left to right along the rows.

(b) Ask the child to give the 'phonic' sounds which these letters stand for.

(c) Ask the child to identify the initial and end letters of words spoken by the tester. Treat each of the five lines as five separate items.

Point to the first line and say 'Which of these letters does the word *man* begin with?'

If he hesitates, point to *c* and say 'Does *man* begin with this letter?'

'No.'

'Does *man* begin with this letter?' (pointing to *h*)

'No.'

'Does *man* begin with this letter?' (pointing to *m*)

'Yes.'

Emphasise the initial consonant when saying the word *man*.

Words to be read out by the tester for initial consonants:

Line 1	man	cup	bus	hat	dog
Line 2	ink	sit	fast	leg
Line 3	axe	king	red	nest
Line 4	egg	jam	win	on
Line 5	top	pig	gun	van

Next test the child's ability to recognise letters at the ends of words. Explain what is required in the same way. Words to be read out for final consonants:

Line 1	rub	fox	plum	
Line 2	bus	had	hill	stuff
Line 3	win			
Line 5	dog	sit	cup	

ASSESSMENT OF THE TEST RESULTS

Method (a) (naming the letters) and Method (b) (giving the 'phonic' names the letters stand for) should only be used rarely. Naming the letters, however, is an important part of learning to read the 'special' words (Reading Standard II). Method (c) gives much more precise information about the child's insight into the significance of letters.

A child may show in Tests 1, 7, 8 or 9 that, although he has grasped the main principles of letters and letter-sounds, he sometimes confuses or forgets one or more particular letters. This test helps to locate these gaps in his knowledge more precisely.

For children at a lower standard, Reading Standard O, linked with Test 6, the test of aural discrimination, Test 5 gives valuable evidence about the child's readiness to proceed on a systematic course like the Phonic Word Method course of the *Royal Road Readers*. If he shows that he is not ready for such a course, it is clear that he needs to be put on a pre-reading course designed to develop those visual, manual and aural skills to a suitable level.

TEST 5

LETTER RECOGNITION

c	h	m	b	x
l	s	d	i	f
r	a	k	n	u
e	j	q	o	w
g	p	t	v	y

TEST 6

AURAL DISCRIMINATION TEST

To whom this Test should be given

(a) Children who score Standard O on the Standard Test of Reading Skill.

(2) Those children who appear to score better on the Standard Test than would be expected from their performance on Test 5—Method (c).

(3) Children who make particular mistakes in initial sounds of words in the Standard Test.

How to give the Test

Place the page of pictures before the child and say 'Have you ever played the game of "I spy with my little eye"? You have? Well! we are going to play it now.'

Cover up all the pictures except the top row. Now say 'What are these pictures of?' Establish the words *man, pig* and *sun*, over-pronouncing the initial consonants slightly. Now say 'Look at these three pictures. Which thing here has a name beginning with *s-s-s*? Point to the picture of it'.

If the child still hesitates or points to the wrong picture, go through the pictures again naming them and repeat the question. After success with *sun* ask the child to point to the thing whose name begins with *m*—then with *p*. (*N.B.*—Pronounce the *p* explosively—try to avoid adding a neutral vowel.)

Repeat with lines 2, 3 and 4, presenting the sounds in the following order—*a c b; j f l; d h n*. (Pronounce *h* as a throaty, unvoiced *ha* with an extended aspiration. Similarly *l* should not be pronounced *lə* but *l-l-l*.)

A child cannot learn to read effectively unless his powers of auditory analysis have been developed to the point where he can succeed with at least 9 out of the 12 items of this test.

Lack of success may be due to slight partial deafness in limited ranges of frequency. If this is suspected, the child should be referred to the Medical Officer. However, a sort of pseudo-deafness is the most common cause. The ability to analyse the spoken word into its component sounds is often thought to grow 'naturally'. It is true that in the life experiences of most children there 'naturally' occur situations which, by requiring such discrimination, train the child to hear. Rhyming games, for example, provide such experiences. But not all children have such 'accidental' educational experiences. Some of the pre-reading activities of children, therefore, should be designed to teach children to make aural analyses of words. The standard books on infant method describe many such games and activities. These may easily be adapted for use with older backward children. For example, 'Morris Cards' are a useful modification of an old card game to help the older backward reader to learn to 'hear' initial sounds in words.[1]

[1] *The Quality of Learning*, R. Morris (Methuen, 1951).

TEST 6

AURAL DISCRIMINATION

TEST 7

DIAGNOSTIC WORD-RECOGNITION TESTS

(A) Phonically simple two- and three-letter words.
(B) Consonantal blends at beginnings of phonically
    simple words.
(C) Consonantal blends at ends of words.
(D) Polysyllabic phonically simple words.
(E) Graded phonically complex words.
(F) Common words with irregular spelling
    ('Special words').
(G) 'Reversible' words.
(H) Nonsense syllables.

Test 7 consists of a battery of eight word-recognition tests—each with its special function. The function of each test, a statement concerning the children to whom each test should be given and notes on the assessment of the results are to be found accompanying each separate test.

How to give the Tests

Open the test page in front of the child and say 'Here are some words. I want you to read them out aloud for me. Read this one.' (*Point to first one*)

'Yes! Now read *across* the page. This one next.' (*Pointing*)

Make a note of all words missed out or read erroneously. If possible write down the errors the child makes.

TEST 7A

WORD-RECOGNITION TEST

(Phonically simple two- and three-letter words)

To whom this Test should be given

(1) Children scoring Reading Standard O, I and II.

(2) Those children who tend to make errors in recognising, or in associating the right sound-value with, certain particular letters.

(3) Children who appear to have difficulty in synthesizing some words from their component parts.

Assessment of the Test Results

All the letters of the alphabet except *q* and *z* are used in these 15 words. The teacher should make a special note of two points:

(1) Is the child able easily to synthesize the words from their component parts?

(2) Are there any particular letters causing the child difficulty? Remedial activities may then be devised to help the child.

if	up	on	van	ten
cut	kit	jug	six	log
rub	had	jam	win	yes

TEST 7B

WORD-RECOGNITION TEST

(Consonantal blends at beginnings of phonically simple words)

To whom the Test should be given

(1) Children of Reading Standard I and II.

(2) Children having difficulty in reading phonically simple words, whatever their Reading Standard.

Assessment of the Test Results

Most of the two- and three-letter consonantal blends found in English are included in this test. The teacher should make a special note of two points:

(1) Is the child finding blending a special difficulty?

(2) Are there any particular blends which are proving specially difficult for the child?

If it is discovered that any blend is giving trouble, it should be dealt with through specially devised activities.

brag	clog	grim	stop	glad	
drop	flag	snap	smell	span	
tram	dwell	frog	bless	plan	swim
skim	crop	slip	prod	strap	sprat

TEST 7c

WORD-RECOGNITION TEST

(Consonantal blends at ends of phonically simple words)

To whom the Test should be given

(1) Children of Reading Standard I and II.

(2) Children having difficulty in reading phonically simple words whatever their Reading Standard.

Assessment of the Test Results

The assessment of the results of this test is identical with that of Test 7B.

help	send	damp	felt	sink	
jump	bent	best	gasp	desk	
rapt	long	dogs	sits	sings	lamps

TEST 7D

❦

WORD-RECOGNITION TEST

(*Polysyllabic phonically simple words*)

To whom the Test should be given

(1) Children of Reading Standards I, II and III.

(2) Children having difficulty in reading polysyllabic words, whatever their Reading Standard.

Assessment of the Test Results

Some children who are fluent readers of mono-syllables (even complex ones) seem to have special problems connected with recognising the syllables composing longer words. This test probes the difficulties of these children. For those children who have a great deal of difficulty in this, the following remedial exercise has been found helpful:

Reading lists of words with a little larger space than ordinary letter space between the syllables followed by reading the same words made up into another list without this adventitious aid. In the second list, the order of the words should to be changed.

picnic	kitten	upon	level	cricket
across	sitting	insect	visit	expect
umbrella	caravan	lifted	undressed	collected

TEST 7E

WORD-RECOGNITION TEST

(Graded phonically complex words)

To whom the Test should be given

Children scoring a reading standard of II, III, IV and V, especially those children who show uncertainty in the recognition of various digraphs.

Assessment of the Test Results

The purpose of this test is to help the teacher to discover (in children of fairly high reading standard) what particular phonic rules have not been grasped, with a view to designing remedial exercises.

chop	ship	witch	mash	thin
bath	foot	mood	heed	fork
dart	herd	bird	turn	gate
these	fine	hope	mule	page
mice	bead	great	deaf	toy	boil

boat	pain	stay	fall	kind	
sty	moor	deer	care	here	
fire	shore	pure	fear	fair	
pear	wild	half	cause	cow	
low	few	down	round	sold	fight

TEST 7F

WORD-RECOGNITION TEST

(*Common words with irregular spelling*)

To whom the Test should be given

Children of Reading Standards II, III, IV and V, especially those who show a tendency to phoneticise common irregularly-spelt words.

Assessment of the Test Results

The experiments reported in *Progress in Reading* have shown that there is an optimum point in a systematic course in reading when common irregularly-spelt words (i.e. 'special' words) are best introduced to the child, namely, when the children have some insight into the principle that letters stand for sounds. A child who scores 12 marks on Test 7A is ready to begin with the simplest 'special' words. A child who achieves Reading Standard III should be able to read 10 'special' words.

I to of who said here go they

where you any came eye eight one

have laugh are no great

TEST 7G

WORD-RECOGNITION TEST

('Reversible' words)

To whom the Test should be given

All children who in any other test read one or more words reversed.

Assessment of the Test Results

It is important to establish early in the child's reading the habit of reading words from left to right. One of the main criticisms that may be directed at the 'Look and Say' theory of teaching reading is that it enables children to establish poor reading habits, including right-left analysis of word structure, in the early stages. The error of 'reversal' reading is partly traceable to poor visual left-right orientation (see pp. 113-114) and partly due to the practice of trying to recognise words by unessential details. Teachers often unwittingly emphasise attacking a word at the end rather than at the beginning when they write words on the black-board and say the word out aloud as they finish the last letter of the word. This association of the word with the last letter can easily develop into a chronic habit of reading words from right to left.

Exercises with words similar to those given in the test are helpful. Exposing these words gradually from left to right often helps. The establishment of good writing habits is, however, perhaps the best cure for this problem.

tub   let   god   dab   net   pots

saw   now   grill   inch   fist   felt

TEST 7H

WORD-RECOGNITION TEST

(Nonsense Syllables)

To whom the Test should be given

This is not one of the tests that should be used frequently. Some teachers may feel, with some justification, that they should never use it at all. There are two types of child with whom this test may be found useful: (1) The very rare, glib reader who pays practically no attention to what he is reading. (2) The child who has mastered the basic skills of reading but who is not sure enough of this principle to permit him to utter 'nonsense'.

Assessment of the Test Results

Many good readers score poorly on this test because they refuse to read 'nonsense'. Two reactions have been noticed: (a) there are those who remain silent and look in a puzzled way into the teacher's face; (b) there are those who guess wildly at the nearest sensible word even though guessing at words is not one of their usual failings. Some children, however, who are only at Reading Standards I and II read these nonsense syllables fluently—apparently unaware that they are reading 'nonsense'. When this happens, steps should be taken to prevent the child from becoming a mere word-caller.

sab   bim   lep   bup   rad   hud

tog   sug   joz   dack   stib   velb

TEST 8

ORAL WORD-RECOGNITION TEST

To whom this Test should be given

(1) Children who have shown in the Standard Test of Reading Skills that they often make wild guesses at words by looking at one or two letters in the words (usually the first or the last letters) and saying any word that begins or ends with these letters.[1]

(2) Children who, though reading tolerably well, appear to have difficulty in picking out the individual sounds in spoken words.

(3) Children who confuse certain pairs of letters, e.g. *b* and *d*.

(4) All children who are given Test 9. (This test is suitable only for children who score Standard I, II, III or IV in the Standard Test.)

How to give the Test

Each line of four words represents one item of the test. The page of words is placed in front of the child. Since he has to point to certain words, the page will be kept cleaner if he is provided with an unsharpened pencil to point with. Say to him—'Look at these four words [*Point*]. Which one of them says *on?*' If he hesitates, point to *on* and say 'Is this *on?*' 'Yes.' 'Point to it, then, with this [*Tap the unsharpened pencil*]. Now which of these says *it?* Point to *it.*' Make a note of the words the child points to from this line onwards.

The complete list of words to be recognised is: *on, it, men, glad, stick, west, camel, across, rabbit, little, gorilla, ride, fed.*

[1] See *Progress in Reading*, p. 45 *et seq.*

ASSESSMENT OF THE TEST RESULTS

The test is concerned with discovering the accuracy and the firmness of the links which teaching has established between his centres of visual analysis and aural analysis.

173

STANDARD READING TESTS

Success in this test depends upon whether the child is:

(1) able to analyse the spoken word into its component sounds and to preserve the order in time;

(2) aware of the letters which symbolise these sounds and able to recognise them in print;

(3) aware of the relation of the left-right order of letters to order in time of the sounds of the words.

Deficiency in any one of these skills will induce failure in the test. A detailed examination of the items which the child fails to answer correctly and of the preferred errors, together with the details of the information given for tests 1, 5, 6, 7A, 7H and 9, will locate the difficulties and suggest remedial activities.

TEST 8

ORAL WORD-RECOGNITION TEST

in	on	no	an
at	if	it	to
men	den	won	new
gilt	glad	drag	yard
stick	ticks	stiff	sting
went	wet	newt	west

lemon	camel	came	candle
acorns	acres	course	across
rapid	rabbit	tit-bit	rubbed
little	ladle	battle	light
grill	vanilla	pagoda	gorilla
reed	rid	red	ride
fade	fed	deaf	sad

PICTURE WORD-RECOGNITION TEST

To whom this Test should be given

(1) Children who show a disposition to guess words from the context.
(2) Children whose word-recognition ability is relatively high but who appear to be 'word-calling'—reading aloud without comprehension.
(3) All children who are given Test 8.

How to give the Test

Place the first page of the test open in front of the child. Provide the child with an unsharpened pencil as a pointer. Now point to the picture of the cat and say 'What is this? . . . Yes—a cat.' (If the child says 'Pussy' or 'pussy-cat' or some similar word, say 'Yes—*cat—cat*'.) 'Now look at these four words [*Pointing to the line of four words*]. One of them is the word *cat*—point to the word *cat* . . . Yes—that's good. This word *cat* could be used as the label or name for this picture, couldn't it? Now look at this picture. Don't tell me what you call it. Just point to the word in these four which could be used as a label or name for this picture.' Proceed through the test in this way, noting the response to each item.

This test is a further development of Test 8. One additional task is involved, in addition to that of recognising what the picture portrays: the child has to make an auditory analysis of the words *spoken silently to himself*. This is by no means the same thing as making an auditory analysis of words articulated very deliberately by the teacher. Children tend more easily under these circumstances to confuse pairs of letter-sounds as *b* and *p*, *j* and *ch*, *t* and *d*, *v* and *z*, and *f*, *s* and *c*, and a whole range of vowel sounds. The information given by this test is supplementary to the information gained from Test 8. The results of the two tests should be studied together.

TEST 9

PICTURE WORD-RECOGNITION

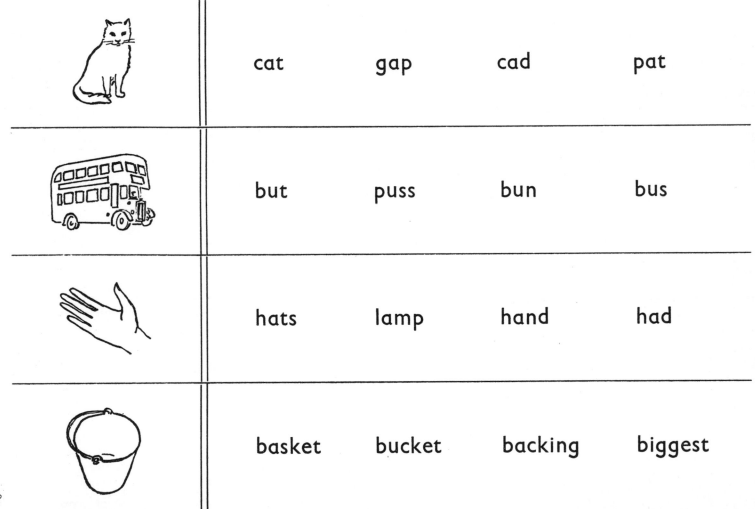

cat	gap	cad	pat
but	puss	bun	bus
hats	lamp	hand	had
basket	bucket	backing	biggest

	revel	camera	caramel	camel
	vista	witch	flash	fish
	spool	moon	spoon	stood
	attract	actor	tractor	sector

lurch	church	chump	churn
spate	speed	spade	pads
lies	first	fir	fire
chill	shield	child	build

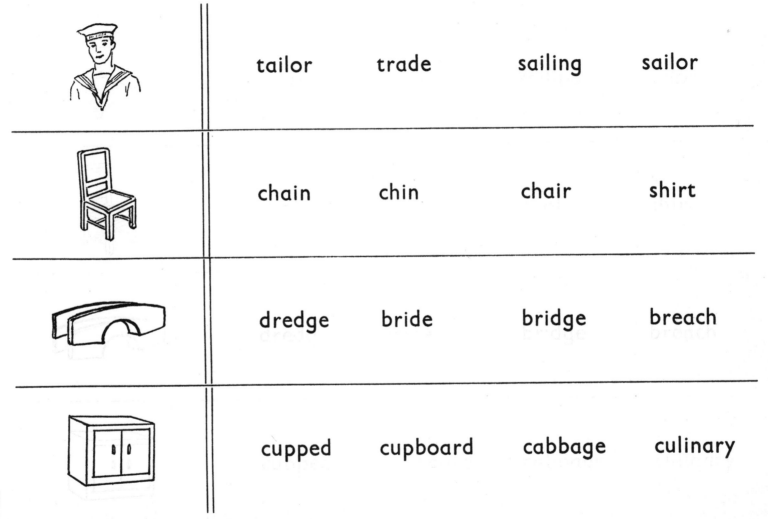

tailor	trade	sailing	sailor
chain	chin	chair	shirt
dredge	bride	bridge	breach
cupped	cupboard	cabbage	culinary

SILENT PROSE-READING AND COMPREHENSION TEST

To whom this Test should be given

The test is about Reading Standard V level. It should be given to those children who reach Reading Standard V or VI on the Standard Test, yet whose independent silent reading appears to be below this level.

Test I demanded an understanding of what was read aloud. This text gives an indication of the extent to which a pupil is getting the meaning out of his silent reading.

How to give the Test

Put the page with the passage on it in front of the child and say 'Read this passage quietly to yourself. Tell me as soon as you have finished reading it. [*On the average, children finish reading the passage after about 3 minutes.*] When you have finished I'm going to ask you some questions about it. So try to remember as much as you can about the passage.'

As soon as the child indicates he has read the passage, turn over the page to the questions and pictures.

Say 'Read this first question [*Pointing*] out aloud to me.'

When he has done this, say 'Now point to the right picture.'

Progress through the test until all ten questions have been attempted. If the child cannot read some of the questions aloud, help him to do so.

ASSESSMENT OF THE TEST RESULTS

Unlike Tests I and 12, no Reading Ages or Reading Standards norms are provided for this Test.

The teacher should make a qualitative assessment of the child's ability to read silently and to comprehend and remember what he has read.

Any child whose performance is much poorer than expected from his score on the Standard Test (he should get at least 5 out of 10 questions right) needs to be encouraged in a practical way to read a lot more interesting material on his own.

TEST 10

SILENT PROSE-READING AND COMPREHENSION TEST

One day John went into the town with his mother in order to buy a new coat. As he was walking down the street he saw a man standing on the edge of the pavement, selling toys. The toys were on a tray which hung from the pedlar's neck by a leather strap. On this tray were small dolls dressed in Welsh costume and a number of small model cars, painted red. John asked his mother whether he could buy a doll for his sister's birthday. His mother replied 'Yes, that is very kind of you.' She took from her purse the money that John had saved out of his pocket-money. She handed the money over to John. John selected a two-shilling piece and gave it to the pedlar. The pedlar took the money and, with a broad smile on his face, handed one of the pretty dolls over to John.

1. Which picture best fits the story you have just read?
2. What colour were the cars the pedlar was selling?
3. What did John buy?
4. Why was John visiting the town with his mother?
5. Where was the pedlar standing?
6. Who was soon to have a birthday?
7. How much did the pedlar charge for a doll?
8. Whose money did John spend to buy the doll?
9. Where did John's mother carry the money?
10. What was the doll wearing?

GRADED SPELLING TEST

To whom this Test should be given

(1) Any child or group of children in the school for whom a spelling test is felt to be necessary.

(2) Those children who, though reading well in the oral and picture word-recognition tests (Tests 8 and 9), are reading rather less well in the word-recognition tests (Test 7).

(3) Children who read better in the nonsense syllables test than would be expected from their performance on the other word-recognition tests.

(4) Those children who make many mistakes in reading due to incorrect phonic rendering of irregular words.

(5) Children in Reading Standard III who are making any type of reversal error (List A only).

How to give the Test

Have the children prepare a sheet of paper numbered 1-40. Tell them that they are going to do a spelling test. Read out the first word ' Number 1—*on*. Write down *on*. The boy sits *on* the table. Spell *on*.'

'Number 2—*not*. Mary has *not* been to school today. *Not*.'

Embody each word as it is presented in a simple sentence.

Give one mark for each word correctly spelt (maximum 40). Add up the marks independently for the four sets A, B, C and D for the purpose of inter-set comparisons. Convert the combined totals into spelling ages.

Converting Raw Scores into Spelling Ages

Look down the column headed *Mark* and find the total number of words the child has spelt correctly. Read off the spelling age in the *Spelling Age* column.

> *Example*: A child spells 19 of the 40 words correctly. His spelling age is 7·1 years. *N.B.*—The figure 7·1 years means $7\frac{1}{10}$ years, *not* 7 years 1 month.

TABLE OF NORMS FOR SPELLING TEST

Mark	Spelling Age	Mark	Spelling Age	Mark	Spelling Age
0	5·0	14	6·5	28	8·2
1	5·2	15	6·6	29	8·3
2	5·3	16	6·7	30	8·5
3	5·4	17	6·8	31	8·7
4	5·5	18	7·0	32	9·0
5	5·6	19	7·1	33	9·2
6	5·7	20	7·2	34	9·5
7	5·8	21	7·3	35	9·8
8	5·9	22	7·5	36	10·2
9	6·0	23	7·6	37	10·5
10	6·1	24	7·7	38	11·0
11	6·2	25	7·8	39	11·6
12	6·3	26	7·9	40	12·3
13	6·4	27	8·1		

Spelling Quotient

If a spelling quotient is wanted, find the child's real (chronological) age (C.A.) in years and tenths of years. Then find the Spelling Quotient (S.Q.) from his Spelling Age (S.A.) from the following equation:

$$\text{S.Q.} = 100 \times \frac{\text{S.A.}}{\text{C.A.}}.$$

Example: A pupil is 7 years 2 months (C.A. = 7·2 years) and scores 9 marks in the spelling test. He thus has a Spelling Age (S.A.) of 6·0 years.

$$\text{S.Q.} = \frac{100 \times 6 \cdot 0}{7 \cdot 2} = 83.$$

The Mean Spelling Quotient is, of course, 100, whilst the Standard Deviation of S.Q.s derived from this test is 15·3.

ASSESSMENT OF THE TEST RESULTS

On the average, a child's spelling age will tend to be equal to his Reading Age as given by Test 1 (Standard Test) and Test 12 (Graded Test of Reading Experience). However, a number of children do appear to have special difficulties with spelling. This is not the place to deal with the teaching of spelling except in so far as it is related to reading. Three types of spelling error are intimately connected with reading difficulties:

(a) Errors due to jumbling the order of the letters (*ship* spelt *hsip*; *also* as *aslo*).

(b) Errors of incorrect rendering of one or more letters related in sounds (*beg* spelt *bec*; *plan* as *blan*).

(c) Errors due to writing irregularly-spelt words in simple phonics.

Treatment for errors of type (c) should be an extension of the methods advocated for teaching children to read 'special' words.

The error of jumbled letters is characteristically an error associated with the child being taught for too long by means of whole-word methods. These children need exercises which emphasise the significance of the order of letters in words.

Children who score reasonably well on the Standard Test and yet have a large number of spelling errors of type (b) (i.e. incorrect rendering of one or more letters) should be given Tests 5c and 6. These tests will help to locate the difficulty and to measure the extent of the confusion. With older pupils errors of letter confusion are difficult to eradicate but the resourceful teacher will find it possible to devise special exercises to help the child to relearn these letters in a realistic way.

TEST 11

GRADED SPELLING TEST

LIST A		LIST B		LIST C		LIST D	
1	on	11	the	21	ship	31	eye
2	hot	12	go	22	food	32	fight
3	cup	13	for	23	fire	33	friend
4	van	14	so	24	thin	34	done
5	jam	15	me	25	date	35	any
6	lost	16	are	26	chop	36	great
7	sit	17	of	27	seem	37	sure
8	plan	18	do	28	dart	38	women
9	mud	19	who	29	loud	39	answer
10	beg	20	here	30	form	40	beautiful

GRADED TEST OF READING
EXPERIENCE

To whom the Test should be given

Children scoring Standard IV, V or VI on the Standard Test of Reading Skill, and especially those children whose performance in the Standard Test leads the examiner to suspect a mechanical approach to reading at the expense of comprehension.

How to give the Test

This is a group test. The test material should be typed and cyclostyled—one question paper for each child. The material just fits two sides of a sheet of foolscap.

Ask the children to fill in personal details asked for at the top of their question papers.

By means of a black-board example explain how the test is to be done:

A bird has two (heads, feathers, tails, <u>wings</u>).

'Which of the four words in brackets makes this into a sensible sentence? A bird has two heads?'

'No!'

'Feathers? Tails? Wings?'

'Yes!'

'*Wings* is the right answer. It has been underlined to show that it is the right answer. In this test you have to answer all the questions in the same way. Underline one word in each set of brackets to make a sensible sentence.'

Give unlimited time, though it will be found that most children will finish within 20 minutes.

Norms

Give one mark for each correct answer, maximum 50.

TABLE OF NORMS

Score	0	1	2	3	4	5	6	7	8	9
0	—	—	—	—	—	—	—	—	—	—
10	6·0	6·1	6·2	6·3	6·4	6·5	6·6	6·7	6·8	6·9
20	7·0	7·1	7·2	7·4	7·5	7·6	7·7	7·8	7·9	8·1
30	8·2	8·3	8·4	8·6	8·7	8·8	9·0	9·1	9·3	9·5
40	9·7	10·0	10·3	10·7	11·2	11·6	12·1	12·6	13·1	13·7
50	14 +									

Example. A child scores 24 in Test 12. Find row 20—move along this row to column 4—Reading Experience Age, 7·5 years.

N.B.—Children who score less than ten marks on this test should not be credited with any Reading *Experience* Age for, at this level, reading tests of this type give highly unreliable estimates of reading ability.

ASSESSMENT OF THE TEST RESULTS

Any child who scores a Reading Experience Age of 9·5 years or more may be said to have mastered the skills of reading and needs no further help in this direction. What the child then has to do in order to develop his reading ability beyond this stage is to read a lot, to read intelligently and to read suitable material. He only needs further reading experience, for he has mastered all the skills.

Reading Ages above 10·0 years are unreliable and misleading. It is easy to produce tests of the same form as Test 12, but containing many more items of greater difficulty, statistically speaking. More difficult questions can be constructed by including long and difficult words, i.e. words used infrequently even in ordinary adult speech and writing, and by choosing questions on topics which require the child to have a knowledge of specialist information. Marks on tests of this type may indeed be significant for the teacher. Such tests, it is known, give fairly accurate estimates of children's ability to do Intelligence Tests, for they measure with reasonable accuracy the global, educational standard of the child. However, because these tests involve many aspects of the child's educational progress other than his skill in reading, they should not be called Reading Tests but rather Reading Comprehension Tests.

A child who scores low marks on Test 12 (i.e. who has a Reading Experience Age below the Reading Age given by the Standard Test of Reading Skill) is meeting some difficulty in comprehending material read silently. What causes such difficulties it is not easy to determine. One of the commonest causes seems to be lack of practice in reading silently for meaning, either to collect information or for enjoyment. A few children, who are rated Standard IV, V or VI in the Standard Test when given at the age of 9, appear to have done little or no independent reading, in school or out of school. If this is continued it can lead to disastrous results. The child who has mastered the skills of reading but who either does not wish, or does not understand how, to utilise the skills must be regarded as backward.

There is only one way of remedying this situation. Children need, right from the start, interesting graded supplementary reading material which they are induced by various incentives to read for themselves. It is also essential to have some method of ensuring that the books are really read. It must, however, be a method which does not make reading a drudgery which the child feels is to be resisted whenever possible.

TEST 12

GRADED TEST OF
READING EXPERIENCE

1. Trains can often be seen standing in a railway (engine, driver, box, station).
2. If you write with a pen, you also need (crayons, money, help, ink).
3. Children go to school in order to (sleep, run, cry, learn).
4. A horse is an animal with four (tails, eyes, legs, ears).
5. People usually go on their holidays to (enjoy, re-imburse, spite, employ) themselves.
6. Coal is usually (yellow, black, white, pink).
7. Boys often like to climb up (bees, tents, trials, trees).
8. The first meal of the day is called (dinner, breakfast, tea, supper).
9. Books are made of (patent, paper, pamper, pepper).
10. Oranges and bananas are both (fronts, fruit, poisonous, animals).
11. Grass is (blue, green, white, red).
12. Before we eat meat, it should be (swallowed, stroked, cooked, crooked).
13. Mr. Smith is limping because, yesterday, whilst getting off the bus, he slipped and twisted his (armlet, neck, ankle, umbrella).
14. Shoes are usually made of (leather, lather, laces, soles).
15. A giant is a (short, tall, thin, hungry) man.
16. Men's socks are usually (matter, stolen, wasted, knitted).
17. Motor-cars are driven along by petrol being exploded inside the (cabin, pump, engine, steering-wheel).
18. When we go out to a friend's house for tea, we often find that the table is already laid with cups and (visitors, sand, sausages, saucers).
19. Most houses in this country today are lit by means of (candles, oil-lamps, electricity, tapers).
20. If the road is very bumpy, a ride on a bus can be very (uncomforting, uncomfortable, uncontrolled, unconverted).
21. Liquids are usually kept in (boxes, fires, drinks, bottles).
22. A steam engine usually runs on (rails, reels, stoves, signals).

23. One of the best ways of keeping healthy is to take plenty of (examination, examples, excitement, exercise).

24. When we send a letter to a friend, it is usual to fold it and put it into an (address, appliance, affluence, envelope).

25. The season of the year when young green buds appear on the trees is called (autumn, spring, winter, October).

26. The typhoon blew so hard that three thousand houses were (destroyed, annoyed, demonstrated, burst).

27. Unless one is very experienced, rock-climbing can be (lucrative, temporary, dangerous, degenerative).

28. A place where talking films are shown is called a (theatre, cinema, gallery, house).

29. A bald man has little (feet, hair, nose, cap) on his head.

30. A male child is called a (boy, girl, dwarf, nuisance).

31. The head teacher granted (permission, presentation, permutation, refusal) for the boy to be absent from school on the day of his brother's wedding.

32. A prisoner usually longs for his (sentence, toleration, serenade, freedom).

33. When people are ill they are often visited by the doctor who prescribes (prevention, disease, radio, medicine) for them.

34. In this country, the commonest fuel used for house fires is (wood, oil, smoke, coal).

35. The case for the prosecution so impressed the Jury that they found the prisoner (dirty, guiltless, wicked, guilty).

36. A mushroom is an edible (fugitive, fungus, parlour, fantasy).

37. We use soap to wash clothes because it helps to remove the (grease, dye, geese, shrubs) from them.

38. If there is one nearby, you should always cross the road at a (pedestal, railway, channel, pedestrian) crossing.

39. The visitor went to the manager's office and politely asked the secretary if he could have an (interruption, extradition, interest, interview) with the manager.

40. If you want to make sure that the plants in your garden will grow well, it is a good plan to sprinkle them with (seeds, roots, fertiliser, worms).

41. When bombs drop on an undefended city, it is almost certain that they will cause a great deal of (demonstration, suspicion, destruction, conservation).

42. A city has a bigger (popularity, population, rainfall, postulation) than a village.

43. The most important female participant in a wedding is the (groomsman, bridegroom, mother, bride).

44. A man who translates the conversation of two people who cannot speak each other's language is called an (interpreter, interloper, annotator, exploiter).

45. Ships sail from port to port, crossing the seas and oceans carrying (mercenaries, mensuration, meridians, merchandise) to all parts of the world.

46. In spring the farmer is often very busy ploughing the fields, in order to make them ready for (stewing, cattle, sowing, grazing).

47. When two armies are engaged in battle, one of the two (adjectives, adversaries, explosions, swords) usually ends up as the victor.

48. The wheels on a motor-car (rotund, retreat, rotate, excavate).

49. When walking in the woods you must be careful not to throw down lighted matches or you may cause a serious (contemplation, conflagration, stipulation, conflict).

50. The explorers who first reached the South Pole found that the intense cold and the fierce blizzards (receded, impressed, impeded, imposed) their progress.

Daniels and Diack.
Diack.
(s) Reading.